T0017003

This book belongs to

_____

Blessed is the [girl]...whose
delight is in the law of the LORD.

PSALM 1:1-2 NIV

A Girl's Guide to
Studying
Her Bible

Elizabeth George

HARVEST HOUSE PUBLISHERS
EUGENE, OREGON

Cover design by Garborg Design Works
Cover image © Awesome_Design (border) / BIGSTOCK; Garborg Design Works, Inc.
Interior design by Chad Dougherty

For bulk, special sales, or ministry purchases, please call 1-800-547-8979.
Email: Customerservice@hhpbooks.com

M This logo is a federally registered trademark of the Hawkins Children's LLC. Harvest House Publishers, Inc., is the exclusive licensee of this trademark.

Previously published as *A Girl's Guide to Discovering Her Bible*

A Girl's Guide to Studying Her Bible

Copyright © 2015 by Elizabeth George
Published by Harvest House Publishers
Eugene, Oregon 97408
www.harvesthousepublishers.com

ISBN 978-0-7369-8746-2 (pbk.)
ISBN 978-0-7369-8747-9 (eBook)

Library of Congress Control Number: 2023930732

Printed in Colombia

23 24 25 26 27 28 29 30 31 / NI / 10 9 8 7 6 5 4 3 2 1

For my precious granddaughters,

> Taylor Zaengle
> Katie Seitz
> Grace Seitz
> Lily Seitz

May you...

> Study the Bible to be wise;
> Believe it to be safe;
> Practice it to be holy.
> Study it through,
>
> > pray it in,
> > work it out,
> > note it down,
> > pass it on.[1]

Contents

1

Discovering Treasure

How God's Word Can Change Your Life

Oh, how I wish I could meet you and see your room or your place! Nothing is as special as your personal space. If you're like most girls, you've probably got lots and lots of cool stuff in your space. And I'm guessing that you have lots of colorful pens, pencils, and markers for drawing, making greeting cards, working on crafts, and writing in your journal.

Well, to this day, I still love and use colored pens and markers. And the M-O-S-T special way I use them is when I am reading my Bible. Here's how it all started.

When I was about your mom's age, I purchased my very first Bible. As I was paying for it, I noticed a glass bowl filled with brightly colored highlighter pens on the checkout counter. On a whim, I reached into that bowl and picked out a gold marker. And I prayed! Maybe it was because I had been a Christian for only three days before buying a Bible, but in my heart I prayed and talked to God:

God, I'm a new Christian, and I don't know anything about You. I'm going to start reading my brand-new Bible tomorrow and mark everything I learn about You, God, with this shiny gold highlighter.

And *then* I spotted a pink highlighter—my favorite color! So I picked it out of the bowl too, and I prayed again:

And God, I don't know anything about being a Christian woman, wife, or mom. When I start reading my new Bible tomorrow, I'm going to mark everything I learn about women and being a woman with my super-special hot-pink highlighter.

And you know what? The next day, I opened up my crisp new Bible, laid out my two new marking pens, and—I discovered treasure! Without knowing it, I was living what the Bible says: If you look for wisdom and understanding and "seek them like hidden treasures," you will find them (Proverbs 2:4).

Discovering Treasure

See for yourself what I found on my *first* day of reading my Bible, on the *first* page, in the *first* book of the Bible, in the *first* verse in the Bible! It was my first marking with my gold pen. If your Bible is handy, open it up to Genesis 1:1.

With your pen or pencil or maybe a highlighter pen, mark what you learn about God in this one verse.

In the beginning God created the heavens and the earth.

What solid fact does this verse reveal about God?

_____

_____

_____

I kept reading and then I found a verse that called for my pink highlighter pen.

Genesis 1:27—With your pen or pencil or highlighter pen (maybe pink?), mark what you learn about yourself as a woman, as a female.

God created human beings in his own image. In the image of God he created them; male and female he created them.

What do you learn about God in this verse?

_____

_____

_____

What do you learn about man and woman?

_____

_____

_____

As a young woman, I'm sure you hear a lot about self-image. But let's think about "God-image" instead. How does this verse help you with the way you can and should view yourself? Or, put another way, how would you complete this sentence?

I am created by _____

and in the image of _____

Got Problems?

Believe me, I know from my own years as a girl and from raising two daughters that the early years are challenging ones. Some days it seems like everything is new and you wonder, "What happened while I was sleeping?!" On other days, all you can think is "I'm bored."

I've heard the heart-cries of thousands of girls, and here are just a few of their questions and problems:

"My brother and sister are driving me crazy!"

"Why do my parents set so many strict rules? I can't do anything fun."

"Why is it so hard to find a friend? Is something wrong with me?"

"I wish Mom would let me choose my own clothes."

"It seems like all my parents do is correct me and nag me about my chores and homework."

Well, here's some good news. No matter what your problem is, God has the help and answers you need. No matter how bad things seem or become, if you are faithful to look to God's Word each day, He has help and answers for your problems. Every time you open your Bible, God gives you:

— instructions on how to live and make right choices

— encouragement and comfort when your heart hurts

— guidelines and wisdom for handling your problems

— strength for dealing with stressful situations

— promises for whatever you worry about

And best of all, you have Him—all of Him—when you read God's Word!

What do you learn about God in the following verses?

Be strong and courageous! Do not be afraid or discouraged. For the LORD *your God is with you wherever you go* (Joshua 1:9).

Be _____

Do not be _____

or _____

For/because _____

Even when I walk through the darkest valley, I will not be afraid, for you are close beside me (Psalm 23:4).

When I _____

I will _____

For/because _____

He heals the brokenhearted and bandages their wounds (Psalm 147:3).

God _____

God _____

Don't be afraid, for I am with you. Don't be discouraged, for I am your God. I will strengthen you and help you. I will hold you up with my victorious right hand (Isaiah 41:10).

Don't _____

Don't _____

God will _____

God will _____

I am convinced that nothing can ever separate us from God's love. Neither death nor life, neither angels nor demons, neither our fears for today nor our worries about tomorrow—not even the powers of hell can separate us from God's love. No power in the sky above or in the earth below—indeed, nothing in all creation will ever be able to separate us from the love of God that is revealed in Christ Jesus our Lord (Romans 8:38-39).

In a few words, what do these verses say about God's love for you?

_____

_____

All Scripture is inspired by God and is useful to teach us what is true and to make us realize what is wrong in our lives. It corrects us when we are wrong and teaches us to do what is right. God uses it to prepare and equip his people to do every good work (2 Timothy 3:16-17).

The source of Scripture _____

The uses of Scripture _____

_____

The end result—God uses it to _____

_____

A Few Facts About the Bible

I hope you are beginning to sense how excited I was when God's Word began to guide me. My Bible wasn't just another book on my shelf that was gathering dust. No, it was alive and real! And the same can be true for you as well.

Here are a few important facts about the Bible:

Fact #1: The Bible is supernatural. It is the Word of God. What does this verse tell you about the Bible?

All Scripture is inspired by God (2 Timothy 3:16).

_____

_____

Fact #2: The Bible is forever. You already know about fads. Clothing styles come and go. Music styles change—and so do hairstyles. Well, God Himself tells us that we can trust 100 percent of His Word. What does this verse tell you about the Bible?

The grass withers and the flowers fade, but the word of our God stands forever (Isaiah 40:8).

_____

_____

_____

Fact #3: The Bible is useful. Read Psalm 19:7-11 and circle each claim the Bible makes for itself, and then underline how it can be useful to you. I have done the first part of verse 7 for you.

7 *The instructions of the LORD are* perfect, *reviving the soul*.

The decrees of the LORD are trustworthy,
making wise the simple.

8 *The commandments of the LORD are right,*
bringing joy to the heart.

The commands of the LORD are clear,
giving insight for living.

9 *Reverence for the LORD is pure,*
lasting forever.

The laws of the LORD are true;
each one is fair.

10 *They are more desirable than gold,*
even the finest gold.

They are sweeter than honey,
even honey dripping from the comb.

11 *They are a warning to your servant,*
a great reward for those who obey them.

Help for Your Life

As you can see from so many verses in the Bible, God has answers and advice for your every need, your every problem. He has help for your life. Here's what Psalm 119:9 says:

How can a young person stay pure? By obeying your word.

According to this verse, how can you avoid problems and stay out of trouble?

_____

_____

Circle the commands (what God tells you to do) in these next two verses.

Like newborn babies, you must crave pure spiritual milk so that you will grow into a full experience of salvation (1 Peter 2:2).

So that _____

_____

Grow in the grace and knowledge of our Lord and Savior Jesus Christ (2 Peter 3:18).

Looking at Your Life

As you think back about the subjects covered in this chapter, I hope you will think about your relationship with Jesus. A sure way to get to know more about Him is to read about His life in the Bible, in the books of Matthew, Mark, Luke, and John. Like the Bible says, knowing Jesus as your Savior gives you joy, purpose, and eternal life.

I hope you will also think about how much you value the Bible. Is it important to you, or not so important? Are you eager to listen to what God has to say to you?

Here's some good news. The more you read the Bible, the more exciting it becomes—and the more answers you will find for your problems. And, of course, the more you will grow to be like Jesus.

Right now, jot down at least one thing you will begin to do after reading this chapter.

I want to start _____

_____

A Prayer for You

It's impossible to count the number of times I've heard Christians say, "I just want to know God." Or I hear them pray, "Lord, I want to know You." These are also the desires of my heart, and I'm guessing yours too!

But knowing God doesn't come from sitting on a mountaintop looking off into space. Knowing God comes from reading what God reveals about Himself in His Word, the

Bible. Read the apostle Paul's prayer for all believers. It is my prayer for you:

> *I pray that your love will overflow more and more, and that you will keep on growing in knowledge and understanding. For I want you to understand what really matters, so that you may live pure and blameless lives until the day of Christ's return* (Philippians 1:9-10).

Now make this your prayer—substitute the words "my" and "I" every time you see "you" and "your" in the verses above.

A Prayer to Pray

> *This is my prayer: that _____ love may overflow more and more in knowledge and understanding, so that _____ may be able to understand what really matters and may live pure and blameless until Christ returns* (Philippians 1:9-10).

First Things First

Making God Your Number One Priority

here are many roads to Jesus, but only one way to God." Have you heard this saying before? And are you wondering what that one way to God is? Well, here's the answer: It is through God's Son, Jesus Christ. It's just like Jesus said in John 14:6—

No one can come to the Father except through me.

Once again I am wishing I could visit with you. I especially wish I could listen to you share how your spiritual journey is coming along. I wonder, have you found out about Jesus? Have you received His gift of forgiveness and salvation and new life? Do you attend church? How has God directed your spiritual growth?

Whatever your path has been, I am so glad God has connected you and me now—today—through this book.

I've already told you a little about my journey toward Jesus and how important the Bible is to me. That is why I am writing this book. I want to encourage you to put first things first, to put God and His Word first. First in your heart. First in your life. First thing each day.

Reality Check

How does your day go? Like all days, it probably starts with a wake-up call, right? Your alarm clock? Your phone alarm? Your "Mom" alarm?

Then, as you crack open your eyes, you begin thinking about all the urgent, important, necessary, and fun things you are facing in your bright new day. It takes only a minute or two for you to realize, "Oops, if I don't cut some things out from my day, I won't get my urgent projects done. I won't finish all my homework. I won't be ready for my test!"

And, believe it or not, right at this point, many girls choose to skip reading the Bible. They think, *I'll have some time to read my Bible later—maybe at lunch or during a break, or maybe tonight when I get in bed.*

And off they go, into the brand-new day God has given them...without checking in with God. Without receiving wisdom from His Word that will help them with their day. Without tuning their heart in to God.

Putting First Things First

Now try out this option. Once you're up, you decide you want to put first things first. You want to choose to make God your Number One priority. You want to meet with Him before another hectic day gets rolling.

Here are a few key verses that show you how important God's Word is.

All Scripture is given by inspiration of God, and is profitable [*useful* NIV] (2 Timothy 3:16 NKJV).

Who is the author of "all Scripture"?

_____

Look up the word "profitable" in a dictionary and write its meaning below:

_____

_____

_____

Now read all of 2 Timothy 3:16 in another Bible translation:

All Scripture is God-breathed and is useful for teaching, rebuking, correcting, and training in righteousness (NIV).

What are the four things God's Word claims it will do for you?

_____

_____

_____

_____

Now read the next verse, 2 Timothy 3:17. What else does God's Word do for you?

God uses it to prepare and equip his people to do every good work.

_____

_____

Without question, anytime you read God's Word, you are doing something profitable.

Just for this week, set a goal to spend five minutes a day reading your Bible. A good place to start is the gospel of Mark. It's fast-paced. And best of all, it's about Jesus. Then note your progress here with a checkmark:

___ Monday   ___ Wednesday   ___ Saturday

___ Tuesday   ___ Thursday   ___ Sunday

                     ___ Friday

Buying Back Time

Are you thinking, "Wow, I'm already super busy! I've got homework, music lessons, and soccer practice. And I love doing all my crafts. How will I find time to also read my Bible?" As always, God has answers for you. Ephesians 5:16-17 (NKJV) says we should be...

...redeeming the time, because the days are evil. Therefore do not be unwise, but understand what the will of the Lord is.

...Make the most of every opportunity in these evil days. Don't act thoughtlessly, but understand what the Lord wants you to do (NLT).

What should you be doing about your time?

_____

Here are a few ways you can be wise and "redeem" or "buy back" time so you can do what's truly important— spend time in God's Word.

— Get up 15 minutes earlier each day. (This means you may have to go to sleep 15 minutes earlier the night before.)

— Decide not to work on your hobbies until you have spent time reading the Bible.

These are just a few examples of how you can buy back time for the most important thing in life—growing in your relationship with God. The Bible is a special book. In fact, it's the greatest book ever written! And if you are a Christian, God's Spirit—the Holy Spirit—speaks to you through God's Word as you read it (John 14:26). That's why it's so important to spend time reading God's Word. When you do,

— you will think differently

— you will live differently

— you will grow spiritually

— you will be blessed

I'm sure you agree that these benefits and blessings are worth the simple effort of getting up a few minutes early so you can make sure you have time to read your Bible.

Count Your Blessings

Blessings abound when you turn to God's Word! Read the following verses and describe how God's Word can help you.

I have hidden your word in my heart, that I might not sin against you (Psalm 119:11).

_____

_____

Your word is a lamp to guide my feet and a light for my path (Psalm 119:105).

_____

_____

My husband and I begin our power walk early each day while it is still dark. So we take a flashlight for safety and guidance. But back when Psalm 119 was written, light was provided by a simple lighted wick in a saucer filled with oil. It was sort of like a candle that provided just enough light for a person to see one step ahead in the dark. Its light kept a person from wandering off the path or tripping on something that could cause an injury.

When it comes to your walk with God, His Word points

the way. It lights your path. It gives you the truth you need to do what is right. As Psalm 23 says, *"He guides me along right paths"* (verse 3).

There are very few things you can be completely sure of. But the Bible is definitely one of them. "All" of the Bible—100 percent of it—is 100 percent from God, 100 percent true, and 100 percent helpful and useful.

So pick up your Bible and get ready to have your world rocked! God's Word is like dynamite—it will definitely change your life.

What else can the Bible do for you? Read about what it did for Timothy:

> You [Timothy] have been taught the holy Scriptures from childhood, and they have given you the wisdom to receive the salvation that comes by trusting in Christ Jesus (2 Timothy 3:15).

_____

_____

_____

Getting into God's Word

Getting into the Bible and having a quiet time alone with God causes you to grow. As you read it, you learn more about God. And as you read it, you grow more like Jesus as you do what He says and follow His example.

Here are a few steps you can take to help you to

understand your Bible and grow to love God's Word more and more. When you take these steps each day, you are making the choice to spend time with God a priority—you are making Him your Number One priority!

Read it. Start anywhere. The only wrong way to read the Bible is not to read the Bible.

Study it. As you continue reading this book, I'll be showing you a few simple steps for how to study the Bible so that it helps you grow spiritually.

Desire it. You already know how important physical food is for your growth and health. Well, you need to view the spiritual food of the Bible as even more important. In the Bible, we read about a man named Job who desired God's Word. He declared, *"I have...treasured his [God's] words more than daily food"* (Job 23:12).

Storing Up Treasure

How can you store up the treasure you discover in your Bible?

Memorize verses from the Bible. Most girls have no problem at all memorizing the lyrics to a favorite song. When I go out, I see girls everywhere listening to their favorite music through their earbuds. They are mouthing the words to the songs they're hearing. Some of them even sing out loud. The words are there in their heads, working through their minds, and coming out of their mouths.

Well, that's how easy and natural memorizing God's

Word can be...if you choose to make it a part of your life. There is no better way to live God's way than to have His Word in your heart and in your mind...and then do whatever God's Word says. If His Word is in your heart, He will use it in your life.

Why memorize Bible verses? To begin, what did God tell Joshua to do and why?

Study this Book of Instruction continually. Meditate on it day and night so you will be sure to obey everything written in it. Only then will you prosper and succeed in all you do (Joshua 1:8).

_____

_____

Just a note: To "meditate" on His Word "day and night" means God expected Joshua to know His Word by heart.

How would this help Joshua? For one thing, it would supply him with the courage needed to lead God's people, the nation of Israel, into battle and into their new homeland—a land filled with hostile enemies. Do you ever need courage? Do you ever need to do something hard?

Knowing God's law would also help Joshua make right choices and serve as a judge among the people. Do you ever need help making right choices?

And here's a big help for Joshua: He may have had a serious problem with fear, and God's Word is loaded with powerful promises that can help us overcome our fears and serve God and His people. Are you ever afraid?

We looked at this next verse earlier, but it's a good reminder. How else does the Bible help you when you memorize Scripture?

> I have hidden your word in my heart
> that I might not sin against you (Psalm 119:11).

The advice to "hide" God's Word in your heart so you don't sin against Him is excellent advice and a forever truth. As a great preacher once noted in his Bible,

> Either this book will keep you from sin,
> or sin will keep you from this book. [1]

Now look above at Psalm 119:11 again. As I studied this verse, I discovered that to "hide" means to store, to treasure. God isn't asking us to gulp His Word down as if it were some awful-tasting medicine that causes us to make a face and say "Ewwww!" No, we are told in Psalm 19:10 that it is sweeter than honey dripping from a honeycomb. And He wants us to *treasure* it and guard it and keep it safe so it's available when we need to pull it out and use it.

Mary Treasured God's Word

Mary, the mother of Jesus, was a young woman who was passionate about memorizing portions of the Bible.

How do we know this? Because when she was just a teenager, she opened her mouth to praise God, and out poured Bible verses—at least 15 references to scriptures from the Old Testament (see Luke 1:46-55).

These were verses and truths Mary had treasured and memorized and stored in her heart. When she opened her mouth, her lips leaked God's Word.

To get started in storing up God's Word in your heart, ask yourself, "What are some of my favorite verses in the Bible?" Pick several. If you know them now, note them here. Or you can choose some verses from this chapter.

_____

_____

Now write one out on an index card and memorize it. Look at it several times a day and try to say it from memory.

If you can't think of a verse, use the two below to get launched. I picked the first one because we all need strength and courage. And I chose the second one to remind us to check with God *before* we make our choices.

Be strong and courageous! Do not be afraid or discouraged. For the LORD your God is with you wherever you go (Joshua 1:9).

Seek his will in all you do, and he will show you which path to take (Proverbs 3:6).

Looking at Your Life

Do you want a more exciting life? Well, you can have it! Just make the choice to pick up your Bible each day, open it up, and take a few minutes to let God speak directly to you. Go on an adventure with Him. Read the stories of His heroes. Learn how His people prayed. See how others handled their problems. And, best of all, get your marching orders for your day straight from the heart of God.

♥ The Best Kind of Studying ♥

If you're a Christian, it makes sense that you'd want to learn as much as you could about Jesus Christ and His Word. Think about it—of all the things you learn in your life, what's the most important? It's not algebra or biology! Although studying these subjects is important and necessary, the most important thing is to know who God is and what He wants you to do in your life. And the more you learn about Him, the more you feel secure and have strength for whatever challenges you have to face. Reading the Bible is the best kind of studying![2]

3

A Girl After God's Heart

Meeting Mary in Luke 1

I absolutely love writing books for girls of all ages—especially those *your* age! My goal in this book is to share Bible verses that help you with your daily life and your problems. I also want to share simple and exciting ways to better understand what the Bible verses are saying. Right now let's turn our focus to what it means to follow after God's own heart. God asks us to follow Him and His ways, and to grow as Christians—to grow in our love for Him.

What Does It Mean to Follow Jesus?

In Matthew 4:19-20, Jesus was looking for people to take His message of salvation to a lost world. Read these verses now and have your favorite pen or pencil ready.

19 *Jesus called out to [some fishermen], "Come, follow me, and I will show you how to fish for people!"*

20 *And they left their nets at once and followed him.*

What was Jesus' command to these fishermen (verse 19)?

_____

_____

What was their response to Jesus (verse 20)?

_____

_____

Jesus asked for a commitment from these men. He asked them to quit their jobs, leave their profession, and trust and follow Him. They didn't have to respond at all, but they did. They chose to leave everything and follow Jesus.

That's the kind of commitment Jesus wants from you. He wants you to desire to follow Him more than you desire anything else. He doesn't want you to follow Him while kicking and screaming. No, He wants you to follow willingly, with your whole heart.

Today we don't follow Jesus physically and literally. We follow Him by learning about Him in the Bible—and doing what He says. As a girl after God's own heart, here are a few decisions you will want to make to grow spiritually:

1. *You will want to read your Bible.* God's Word is where you meet with God. It's where you learn from Him and about Him. God is not going to force you to spend time with Him. No, this is your decision. It's a choice *you* have to make.

Are you wondering, *How can I spend time with God?* Well, think about this: How much time do you spend talking with your friends, watching television, reading your favorite books, or working on crafts? You could take some of this time and choose to spend it with God.

2. *You will want to talk to God.* God speaks to you through His Word, the Bible, and you speak to God through your prayers. Think of prayer as simply talking to God. You talk to your girlfriends, don't you? Well, God is your friend too. And He can help you make the right kind of choices. So pray. Talk to God. Tell Him everything! Share all your problems with Him. Then ask for His advice and help.

3. *You will want to confess your sins.* Here's an important verse about sin.

If we confess our sins to him, he is faithful and just to forgive us our sins and to cleanse us from all wickedness (1 John 1:9).

What does this verse say you are to do?

_____

_____

_____

What does this verse say God will do?

_____

_____

Confession, or admitting you did something wrong restores your relationship with God.

4. You will need to make some sacrifices. Nothing of any worth happens without effort. You already know that. You don't get good grades by doing nothing, do you? No, you study hard and work hard in order to get good grades.

Living the way God wants you to live calls for sacrifice and commitment. It's a little like joining a sports team or enrolling in gymnastics or taking music lessons. You expect to make some sacrifices—like your time, and missing out on other activities. Well, God is asking for this same kind of commitment!

So, what activities would you be willing to scale back on or give up in order to gain something greater—to grow in your spiritual life? Would you be willing to...

　...say no to some time watching television?

　...say no to some time with friends?

　...say no to some time spent on hobbies?

Jesus said, _"If any of you wants to be my follower, you must give up your own way, take up your cross, and follow me"_

(Matthew 16:24). List the three actions Jesus asks of those who follow Him, of those who "come after" Him.

He must _____

and _____

and _____

♥ Learning About Observation ♥

What is OBSERVATION? *Observation* means taking a good look at something. It is one of the skills we use to study the Bible. Here are some important principles of observation. Keep them in mind as you read and study your Bible. Whenever you read your Bible, ask and answer these key "WH" questions:

WHO are the people? If a pronoun (such as "he" or "she") is used, read backward to find their names or information about them. How are they described? Is any information given regarding their family heritage?

WHAT did the people do? Or,

WHAT's happening? Is someone teaching? If so, what are they teaching? Is it a miracle? If so, what happened? Is it a battle? An argument or debate? If so, who is winning? Is it a journey? If so, who's going where...and why?

WHERE did this event or scene take place? Is a country, area, or town mentioned? Is it indoors or outdoors?

Are any specific places named? A field? A garden? A house? Heaven?

WHEN did this event take place? Is a day of the week mentioned? Is the time of day morning, noon, afternoon, or night?

WHY did these people do what they did? (This may or may not be directly stated.) Is someone suffering? Sick? Disabled? Afraid? Are they obeying God? Disobeying God?

Now let's try out your observation skills. I want you to look again at Mary. She shows us what it means to be a girl after God's own heart—a girl who follows God with all her heart.

As you read through each verse that follows, ask and answer the observation questions and make notes in the spaces provided. Not every question asked will be answered in the verses you are looking at. If at first this is a little challenging, don't get discouraged. And don't give up. Just enjoy the story.

Meet Mary—Luke 1:26-38

Oh, how I love this girl! And you will too. This scene from Mary's teenage years shows you what it means to follow God with all your heart. As you begin, pray this prayer from Psalm 119:18: *"Open my eyes to see the wonderful truths in your instructions."*

26 *In the sixth month of Elizabeth's pregnancy, God sent the angel Gabriel to Nazareth, a village in Galilee,*

WHO are the people mentioned, and how are they described?

_____

_____

WHAT's happening?

_____

WHERE: What places are mentioned?

_____

WHEN: What references to time are recorded?

_____

_____

27 *to a virgin named Mary. She was engaged to be married to a man named Joseph, a descendant of King David.*

WHO are the people mentioned, and how are they described?

_____

_____

_____

WHAT's happening?

_____

_____

28 *[The angel] Gabriel appeared to her and said, "Greetings, favored woman! The Lord is with you!"*

WHO are the people mentioned, and how are they described?

_____

_____

WHAT's happening?

_____

_____

29 *Confused and disturbed, Mary tried to think what the angel could mean.*

WHO are the people mentioned, and how are they described?

_____

_____

WHAT's happening?

_____

_____

30 *"Don't be afraid, Mary," the angel told her, "for you have found favor with God!*

WHO are the people mentioned, and how are they described?

_____

_____

WHAT's happening?

_____

_____

31 *You will conceive and give birth to a son, and you will name him Jesus.*

WHO are the people mentioned, and how are they described?

_____

_____

WHAT's happening?

_____

_____

WHEN: What references to time are recorded?

_____

_____

32 *He will be very great and will be called the Son of the Most High. The Lord God will give him the throne of his ancestor David,*

WHO are the people mentioned, and how are they described?

_____

_____

WHAT's happening?

_____

_____

WHERE: What places are mentioned?

_____

_____

WHEN: What references to time are recorded?

_____

_____

33 *and he will reign over Israel forever; his Kingdom will never end!"*

WHO are the people mentioned, and how are they described?

_____

_____

WHAT's happening?

_____

_____

WHEN: What references to time are recorded?

_____

_____

34 *Mary asked the angel, "But how can this happen? I am a virgin."*

WHO are the people mentioned, and how are they described?

_____

_____

WHAT's happening?

_____

_____

35 *The angel replied, "The Holy Spirit will come upon you, and the power of the Most High will overshadow you. So the baby to be born will be holy, and he will be called the Son of God.*

WHO are the people mentioned, and how are they described?

_____

_____

WHAT's happening?

_____

_____

WHEN: What references to time are recorded?

_____

_____

36 *What's more, your relative Elizabeth has become pregnant in her old age! People used to say she was barren, but she has conceived a son and is now in her sixth month.*

37 *For the word of God will never fail."*

WHO are the people mentioned, and how are they described?

_____

_____

WHAT's happening?

_____

_____

WHEN: What references to time are recorded?

_____

_____

38 *Mary responded, "I am the Lord's servant. May everything you have said about me come true." And then the angel left her.*

WHO are the people mentioned, and how are they described?

_____

_____

WHAT's happening?

_____

_____

Making It Personal

Now that you have observed Luke 1:26-38, your next step is to make this passage personal. This step in Bible study is called APPLICATION. Here's what you can learn from Mary's life:

Key Lesson

Mary's trust in God is a lesson on faith. By the age of 12 to 14, Mary had already learned to trust in God and in His Word. As a young girl, what are you doing to cultivate your faith—your trust in God? Or what do you need to do to cultivate your faith and trust in God?

_____

_____

A Verse to Remember

Trust in the LORD with all your heart; do not depend on your own understanding (Proverbs 3:5).

♥ How Do You Respond to God? ♥

God is able to do the impossible. Our response to His demands should not be laughter, fear, or doubt but willing acceptance.[1]

Looking at Your Life

God knows what you are experiencing right now, and He knows what you will experience in the future. He has given you a guidebook, the Bible, to help you every step of the way. The Bible will make you wise unto salvation. And it will serve as a lamp that guides your steps along the road ahead.

So dig into God's Word! Spend time with Him. Talk to Him. And follow Him with all your heart.

A Prayer to Pray

Lord, I want to know You—as my Savior and my Redeemer. I know I don't always act like it, but I want to follow You with all my heart. I know Your Word holds all the answers to my questions and tells me how to live each day. I want to be like Mary. No matter what You ask of me, help me to answer positively and heartily as she did: "I am the Lord's servant... I am willing to do whatever he wants" (Luke 1:38 TLB) and to live out Your will for my life. Amen.

True Beauty

Meeting Esther in Esther 1–4

Have you ever wondered, "Who is the most beautiful woman who ever lived?" When people ask a question like this, they are usually thinking of a woman's physical beauty. You know—they're thinking about a woman with perfect hair, perfect skin, a perfect face, perfect nails, and, of course, a perfect body. They may even think of some woman from the past, like Cleopatra, as the most beautiful woman ever. You have probably watched some beauty pageants on TV or online—like Miss America, Miss Teen USA, or Miss Universe. The women in these pageants are definitely beautiful!

But here's the truth: The most beautiful woman who ever lived was the first woman who ever lived, Eve. She was beautiful because God created her Himself (Genesis 1:27). God created Eve as the perfect woman to be placed in a perfect world. Physically, she was the only perfect woman of all time.

But Eve's beauty was more than skin-deep. She also had

inner beauty because she was sinless. Her heart and life were perfectly pure. She always said the right thing, acted the right way, and was a perfect woman.

Tragically, though, Eve lost her perfect inner beauty when she decided to sin, to do the only thing God told her not to do. Sure, for a while Eve was still beautiful. But because sin had entered the world, her physical beauty began to fade as she grew old and died.

Meet Esther

In this chapter you will meet Esther, a young woman who was not only extremely gorgeous but is also an example for women of all ages of what true beauty is.

As you read through a portion of Esther's story, remember to ask and answer the "WH" questions:

WHO are the people, and how are they described?

WHAT did the people do? Or, WHAT's happening?

WHERE did this event or scene take place?

WHEN did this event take place?

WHY did these people do what they did?

Whatever you do, don't get discouraged. And don't give up. Just enjoy the story of Esther—and learning from Esther. At this time in her life, she was just a little older than you are!

Read the verses that follow and use your pen to answer a few key questions that will teach you more about Esther.

Queen Vashti gave a banquet for the women in the royal palace of King Xerxes (Esther 1:9).

What two key people do you meet in this verse?

_____

_____

Summary: In Esther 1:10-11, we learn that when King Xerxes was drunk, he commanded Queen Vashti to attend the men's banquet so he could show off her beauty.

Queen Vashti...refused to come. This made the king furious, and he burned with anger (Esther 1:12).

What was Queen Vashti's response to the king's command?

_____

What effect did Queen Vashti's response have on the king?

— _____

— _____

Summary: In verses 13-21, we discover that Queen Vashti was removed as queen. Soon a massive search was made for the most beautiful young girls in the Persian Empire. These young women were to be brought to the king's palace and given every kind of beauty treatment. Then the king would choose the young woman who pleased him the most and make her his new queen so he could show off her beauty. But...

What do you learn about Esther in Esther 2:7?

[A Jewish man named Mordecai] had a very beautiful and lovely young cousin, Hadassah, who was also called Esther. When her father and mother died, Mordecai adopted her into his family and raised her as his own daughter.

Her cousin's name was _____

Esther's two names were _____

and _____

How is Esther's appearance described?

_____

_____

Esther may have been taken away from her home and family and friends and placed in a strange place with people she didn't know, but God was with her every step of the way. Read on to discover how God used one person inside the palace to help and take care of Esther.

As a result of the king's decree, Esther, along with many other young women, was brought to the king's harem at the fortress of Susa and placed in Hegai's care. Hegai was very impressed with Esther and treated her kindly. He quickly ordered a special menu for her and provided her with beauty treatments. He also assigned her seven maids specially chosen from the king's palace, and he moved her and her maids into the best place in the harem (Esther 2:8-9).

What was Hegai's position and job?

_____

_____

What did Hegai do for Esther, and why?

_____

_____

_____

_____

Esther 2:12 describes the ultimate beauty treatment!

Before a young woman's turn came to go in to King Xerxes, she had to complete twelve months of beauty treatments prescribed for the women, six months with oil of myrrh and six with perfumes and cosmetics (NIV).

After one year of beauty treatments, each girl was given whatever she asked to wear before the king (verse 13). This included expensive clothes and even jewelry. Most Bible scholars believe each girl was allowed to keep whatever she wore to appear before the king.

When it was Esther's turn to go to the king, she accepted the advice of Hegai, the eunuch in charge of the harem. She asked for nothing except what he suggested, and she was admired by everyone who saw her (Esther 2:15).

If you could ask for anything—and you knew you could keep it—what would you ask for, or what do you think most girls would ask for?

_____

_____

What did Esther do instead?

_____

_____

Whose advice did she choose to take?

_____

_____

What was the result?

_____

_____

Esther Is Made Queen

Think about it—Esther was probably a young teenager around 13 or 14 years old when she was taken away from her home, family, and friends. Many beautiful girls from 127 provinces or states of Persia were rounded up (Esther 2:3) and placed into the king's harem of women. But Esther was one of God's people, and God is always at work in His people's lives—through people, events, and circumstances.

So far, you have met some of the *people* in this story, including Mordecai (Esther's cousin) and Hegai (the man in charge of the king's harem). You have learned about the initial life-changing *event* in Esther's young life—she was carried away from all that was familiar and forced into a scary and undesirable situation. And you have seen her *circumstances*: She had no control over what was happening to her. Now read on about the next *event* that took place.

The king loved Esther more than any of the other young women. He was so delighted with her that he set the royal crown on her head and declared her queen instead of Vashti. To celebrate the occasion, he gave a great banquet in Esther's honor for all his nobles and officials, declaring a public holiday (Esther 2:17-18).

What was the result of Esther's decision to ask for nothing except what was advised by Hegai—the one person who knew what the king would like?

_____

_____

How did the king honor Esther?

_____

_____

Wow—what a story! We have talked about beauty and beauty pageants and competitions. But in Esther, we see it for real. Does it sound glamorous? Exciting? Like a dream come true? Like a "princess movie" you have watched?

Well, God always has a purpose for His people—including you! And He had a grand purpose for Queen Esther.

Esther to the Rescue

What do you learn about Esther and her cousin Mordecai in the following verses?

At that time there was a Jewish man in the fortress of Susa whose name was Mordecai son of Jair. He was from the tribe of Benjamin (Esther 2:5).

Mordecai: _____

_____

Esther had not told anyone of her nationality and family background, because Mordecai had directed her not to do so (Esther 2:10).

Esther: _____

_____

Mordecai and Esther were Jews—they were God's people. And they were both positioned inside the king's citadel. And for what purpose? To save God's people, the Jews!

Summary of Esther 2:19–4:8: When an evil man named Haman convinced the king to kill all the Jews in the 127 provinces under the king's rule, Mordecai went into action. He sent a messenger to Esther to

explain the situation to her. He also asked...her to go to the king to beg for mercy and plead for her people (Esther 4:8).

What did Mordecai ask Esther to do?

_____

_____

Esther told [the messenger] to go back and relay this message to Mordecai: "All the king's officials and even the people in the provinces know that anyone who appears before the king in his inner court without being invited is doomed to die unless the king holds out his gold scepter. And the king has not called for me to come to him for thirty days" (Esther 4:10-11).

What was the problem? Why did Esther think she could not do as Mordecai asked?

_____

_____

_____

_____

Mordecai sent this reply to Esther: "Don't think for a moment that because you're in the palace you will escape when all other Jews are killed. If you keep quiet at a time like this, deliverance and relief for the Jews will arise from some other place, but you and your relatives will die. Who knows if perhaps you were made queen for just such a time as this?" (Esther 4:13-14).

What did Mordecai ask Esther to do, and why?

_____

_____

The most famous words in the book of Esther are found in Esther 4:15-16. They appear in **bold** text below:

*Then Esther sent this reply to Mordecai: "Go and gather together all the Jews of Susa and fast for me. Do not eat or drink for three days, night or day. My maids and I will do the same. And then, though it is against the law, I will go in to see the king. **If I must die, I must die.**"*

What did Esther ask the Jews to do before she went before the king, and for how long?

_____

_____

How did Esther prepare herself before she went before the king, and for how long?

_____

_____

Summary of the remainder of the book of Esther: Esther is a thrilling book, and in Esther, the woman, we see what true beauty of character looks like and what it means to trust God. What happened next?

— Esther went before the king and invited him to two dinners.

— Esther appealed to the king: *"If I have found favor with the king, and if it pleases the king to grant my request, I ask that my life and the lives of my people will be spared. For my people and I have been sold to those who would kill, slaughter, and annihilate us. If we had merely been sold as slaves, I could remain quiet..."* (Esther 7:3-4).

— A royal edict to kill the Jews had already been sent out across the land, stating the slaughter would occur on a specific date. Because a royal edict could not be changed, the king issued a new edict that allowed the Jews to fight back and defend themselves—which they did with great success. It has been evident to all throughout history that Mordecai's words were true: Esther *was "made queen for just such a time as this"* (Esther 4:14). God's people were saved!

Looking at Your Life

There's no doubt that Esther was beautiful—inside and out. She was truly a display of a multitude of character qualities. Think back on her story. Then list two or three character qualities you admire in her and want to be evident in your life.

_____

_____

_____

A Prayer to Pray

God, even though You are not mentioned in the book of Esther, Your presence and Your purposes are seen. Thank You that You take such good care of Your people. Help me to be an Esther—a young woman full of faith and courage, one who trusts in You. I want to focus more on what's inside my heart and less on what I look like or what people think of me. I need to spend more time looking up at You, God, than I spend looking in a mirror. Amen.

5

Gaining Wisdom

A Study on Proverbs 31:1-9

I am really glad you are going with me on the journey we are taking in this book. I am also glad to be sharing passages from the Bible that are just for you as a growing girl. By learning to observe what the Bible says and asking and answering questions, you can now discover what a verse or passage says.

Are you ready to take another step? To discover more treasure? Let's venture into what is sometimes called the "wisdom literature" of the Bible. This wisdom literature includes five books that are located near the middle of your Bible. They are:

Job

Psalms

Proverbs

Ecclesiastes

Song of Solomon

Many books of the Bible deal with information and history. But the five wisdom books say a lot about how you can love God and worship Him, how you can praise and pray to Him. And whenever you are suffering or hurt or confused or need to make a tough decision, these books of wisdom come to your rescue with answers and guidance.

Most of all, these five books give you *wisdom*—just what you need to help you make the best choices and decisions each day!

To get a taste of what is found in the wisdom books, let's take a look at Proverbs 31. In this chapter you will meet God's ideal woman, also known as "the Proverbs 31 woman." Now, grab your Bible. You'll be using it. And here we go—enjoy!

Proverbs 31:1-9

1 *The sayings of King Lemuel contain this message, which his mother taught him.*

Who are the two people mentioned in this verse?

Person #1: _____

Person #2: _____

Just a note: The name "Lemuel" means "dedicated to God" or "devoted to God."

What message is the man sharing? _____

_____

What did the woman do? _____

_____

Read 2 Timothy 1:3-5 in your Bible. Paul is writing to Timothy. Who are the two women who taught God's Word to Timothy and helped ground his faith in Christ, and how were they related to Timothy (verse 5)?

_____

_____

Read 2 Timothy 3:15. When did Timothy begin to learn God's Word, the Scriptures?

_____

What is one purpose of the Word of God that became real in Timothy's life?

_____

Conclusion: Based on these three passages, what is one key role God gives to godly mothers, and why is it so important?

_____

_____

Personal application: Do you have a mom or grandmom who is trying to teach you truths from the Bible? Who encourages you to have daily devotions or a quiet time? If so, check when you have done the following:

_____ Thank God for her, and

_____ Thank her!

How about an attitude check? Do you make it hard or easy for your parents to talk about the things of God? Do you dread or grumble every time they want to read from the Bible or a devotional book together as a family? Do you murmur? Complain? Whine? Sulk? Drag your heels? Clam up? Act like you are taking some bitter medicine?

Here are some things to think about: Why would a girl your age resent a mother who is doing what the Bible says a godly mother should do? Why should any girl want to "punish" Mom with a bad attitude when all she is doing is obeying God's instructions to her as a mother?

Join your parents' team. Do your part when it's Bible time. Participate in discussions about devotions and family time. Show your brothers and sisters a good example of a listener and a learner. And pray that whatever your mom or parents are teaching you will, as 2 Timothy 3:15 says, *"make you wise to accept God's salvation by trusting in Christ Jesus"* (TLB).

Returning to Proverbs 31, let's look at verse 2 (NIV):

2 *Listen, my son! Listen, son of my womb! Listen, my son, the answer to my prayers!*

What words are repeated three times?

(verb) _____

(noun) _____

Write out a dictionary definition of the word *listen*.

_____

_____

_____

How does this mother describe her relationship to her son, her child?

_____

_____

_____

Personal application: Think about how passionate this mother is about teaching and preparing her child for life. Then think about yourself. How do you respond when one of your parents wants to tell you something? Do you listen—really listen? Do you stop what you are doing and turn toward them, watch their face, stop thinking your own thoughts, and really pay attention?

What changes do you need to make in your attitude

when your parents tell you something that will make your life better?

_____

_____

_____

Believe me when I say that *you*, dear daughter, are precious and priceless to your parents. *You* were passionately wanted and anticipated. *You* are the subject of their most fervent prayers. Count on it, whether your parents say it often or not.

3 *Do not waste your strength on women, on those who ruin kings.*

Now we hear this mother's heartfelt instruction. Are you wondering why we are studying what a mom told her son, her boy? Keep in mind that she is leading up to verse 10, where she tells him what kind of woman to look for and marry.

But first, she instructs him in how to be a godly leader who follows God. After all, he will become a king someday.

What is the first warning this mother gives to her son?

_____

_____

_____

What does she say will happen if her son does not listen to this warning?

_____

_____

Bonus questions—Instead of spending time with many women, what does 1 Timothy 3:2 say a godly leader is to do?

_____

_____

What guidelines do these verses give you in this area of purity and godliness?

1 Timothy 2:9 _____

_____

Titus 2:5 _____

4 *It is not for kings, O Lemuel, to guzzle wine. Rulers should not crave alcohol.*

What is the next topic this mother addresses?

_____

What advice does this mother give to her young son?

_____

_____

Bonus question—What do these verses from Proverbs say are some of the effects of alcohol?

Proverbs 20:1: _____

_____

Proverbs 21:17: _____

_____

Proverbs 23:21: _____

_____

5 *For if they drink, they may forget the law and not give justice to the oppressed.*

What does this wise mom tell her son could happen to him as a leader if he drinks too much?

_____

_____

6 *Alcohol is for the dying, and wine for those in bitter distress.*

7 *Let them drink to forget their poverty and remember their troubles no more.*

Verse 6: Who could benefit from the effects of alcohol?

_____

_____

_____

Verse 7: How could alcohol help those who were suffering and dying?

_____

_____

_____

_____

8 *Speak up for those who cannot speak for themselves; ensure justice for those being crushed.*

9 *Yes, speak up for the poor and helpless, and see that they get justice.*

What role and responsibility does a leader have and for whom?

Verse 8: _____

_____

_____

_____

_____

Verse 9: _____

_____

_____

_____

_____

Personal application: You are not a king and not a political leader. But, like Jesus, you are to be compassionate and helpful and merciful to those who are suffering and in need. Share some ways you usually reach out to help others in need—especially at home.

_____

_____

_____

♥ How Can You Know What to Do...or Not Do? ♥

Here are several questions you can ask yourself that will help you know what to do...and not do:

1. Will it please God? Avoid anything that the Bible says you are not to do. Also be sure to do what the Bible says you should do.

2. Will it help me? Think about it: Is the activity you are considering helpful to you? Is it good for your health and your spiritual growth?

3. Will it hurt someone else? Imagine what it would be like to be in that person's shoes.[1]

Looking at Your Life

It's absolutely true—"A picture is worth a thousand words." And God is giving you a picture of His kind of woman in Proverbs 31, a wise woman and a model for you to follow. As you pause and look at your life, here are a few takeaway truths from Proverbs 31:1-9:

— Your parents: Be glad and pay attention when they give you advice and instructions.

— Your standards: Begin setting them now. Decide what you will and will not do. Be sure and talk them over with your parents.

— Your input: Stay close to God by staying in His Word. Time in your Bible will prepare you to make wise choices all day long.

— Your heart: Be a blessing to others by being compassionate, merciful, and helpful. As Colossians 3:14 says, "*above all, clothe yourselves with love.*"

A Prayer to Pray

Lord, thank You for my parents. Help me to listen to them, ask for their advice, and help them without being told. May I also please You with my actions and choices. With Your help, I want to make this change in my life:

_____

_____

6

Developing Priceless Character

A Study on Proverbs 31:10-20

*H*ave you ever watched a favorite TV program and just when you got to what should have been the end of the program, you saw the words "To Be Continued"?

Well, this chapter is "continued" from the previous chapter. In it we began making our way through the entire chapter of Proverbs 31. This chapter in the Bible will shape your life forever as a woman. And it is taught by a woman who is a strong model of what a woman after God's own heart looks like and what she does. The woman in Proverbs teaches us and shows us how God wants us to live our lives.

So far, you have met a godly mother who was teaching her young son how to be a good leader. She was shaping and preparing him for his future.

Now let's join her again in verse 10. Here this wise mom begins to teach her boy how to find the right kind of wife. She creates a list of qualities an excellent wife would possess.

A Look at God's Picture

Let's begin our look at this life-changing and life-shaping picture of the woman we want to be. Pause, ask God to open your eyes and your heart to His truths, and thank Him for a role model to last you for a lifetime!

Proverbs 31:10-20

10 *Who can find a virtuous and capable wife? She is more precious than rubies.*

What kind of woman is most important to find?

_____

A few Bible facts—Bible reference books tell us that the Hebrew word for "virtuous" or "noble" or "excellent" is used 200-plus times in the Old Testament to describe an army of men, men of war, and men prepared for war.

This Old Testament word means "able, capable, mighty, strong, valiant, powerful, efficient, wealthy," and "worthy."[1]

Conclusion—Mental toughness and physical energy are a part of the makeup of God's Proverbs 31 woman.

Look again at Proverbs 31:10. How does it describe this woman's worth?

_____

Conclusion—Our role model in Proverbs 31 is priceless. She is a noble, excellent, virtuous woman of character, rare and more valuable than all the treasure in the world.

11 *Her husband can trust her, and she will greatly enrich his life.*

Because of this woman's many character qualities, what are two blessings her husband enjoys?

— _____

— _____

12 *She brings him good, not harm, all the days of her life.*

How else does this excellent woman and wife bless her husband?

_____

_____

For how long? _____

Personal application—As a young woman who isn't married yet, realize that the quality we are admiring here in the Proverbs 31 woman is her faithfulness. You too, at your age today, are to have this quality. How do you measure up in this area of faithfulness? Or put another way, how would those who know you best—your family, friends, and schoolmates—rate your faithfulness? Are there any changes you need to make?

_____

_____

_____

13 *She finds wool and flax and busily spins it.*

In the Proverbs 31 woman's day and age, what kind of work did she participate in?

_____

What do you learn about her work ethic and her attitude toward her work?

_____

Personal application and an attitude check—How do you respond to the work you have to do—your schoolwork, your homework, your chores? When Mom asks you to do something or to help out with your brother or sister, how do you respond? Is it, "Oh, no! Why me? Do I have to do it now? Oh, a-l-l right"?

Work is a fact of life. There are many things you must do each day. You have no power over most of them—you simply must do them. But your attitude is always your choice. Write out Colossians 3:23. Then write it out on an index card and carry it with you so you can remember what it says.

_____

_____

_____

According to Colossians 3:23, what is the key to doing your work with a happy heart?

_____

_____

14 *She is like a merchant's ship, bringing her food from afar.*

Oh boy—shopping trip! How is the Proverbs 31 woman described in this verse?

_____

In Proverbs 31, verse 13, this woman shopped for materials to make clothing. In verse 14, what is she seeking?

_____

Personal application—Do you help watch over a younger brother or sister? Are you asked to help with dinner or cleanup? Do you have to practice an instrument? Take care of your clothes? Make a list of your daily duties and responsibilities.

_____

_____

_____

What is your general attitude toward these duties?

_____

_____

_____

Write out some changes you can make so you can do your work with the energy and joy the Proverbs 31 woman models for you.

_____

_____

_____

15 *She gets up before dawn to prepare breakfast for her household and plan the day's work for her servant girls.*

What do you learn about this woman's personal daily schedule?

_____

What was one reason for this daily habit?

_____

Who benefited from this habit?

_____

_____

Personal application—What would happen if you got up just a little earlier each day? What could you get done that you should do? What could you get done that you want to do? Make a list, and try getting up earlier each day for a week.

_____

_____

_____

16 *She goes to inspect a field and buys it; with her earnings she plants a vineyard.*

There is no end to this lady's energy! What else does she do to benefit her family?

_____

_____

How did she pay for her ventures?

_____

17 *She is energetic and strong, a hard worker.*

What do you learn about our role model's work ethic and physical condition and energy?

_____

_____

Bonus question—What resources are available to motivate you as you approach your work?

Nehemiah 8:10—_____

Proverbs 14:23—_____

Philippians 4:13—_____

Personal application—What one thing will you do this week to increase your physical energy? Do you need more sleep? Do you need to add some kind of physical activity to your schedule? Do you need to change your diet and eat foods that give you healthy energy and stamina, and give up the foods that bring you down, that make you want to take a nap? Think about it and write down your one thing.

_____

_____

18 *She makes sure her dealings are profitable; her lamp burns late into the night.*

What result does our Proverbs 31 woman realize from her hard work and diligent efforts?

_____

What decision did she make about her time after seeing good results from her efforts?

_____

What are your favorite hobbies? Are you into crafts? Has God blessed you with a talent? Jot down several answers here.

_____

_____

Now figure out a way to find time for your hobbies.

19 *Her hands are busy spinning thread, her fingers twisting fiber.*

This is probably what the Proverbs lady was doing with her evenings.

Conclusion—What do you usually do with your evenings? Can you think of better choices you could be making for how you spend your time during the evenings?

_____

_____

_____

20 *She extends a helping hand to the poor and opens her arms to the needy.*

God's excellent woman was a hard worker, diligent, and the manager of her home and finances. And in verse 20, we see another part of her character. What two things do you see her doing in this verse?

— _____

— _____

Bonus questions—Take a quick look at another woman of character in 2 Kings 4:8-11. Many people have needs, but not everyone notices them. Who noticed the prophet Elisha and his need?

_____

_____

Sometimes when people do notice someone who has a need, they don't act on it. What did this noble woman in 2 Kings 4 do about the need that she noticed?

_____

_____

Personal application—Our lessons on the Proverbs 31 woman are "To Be Continued." But before you go, pray. Ask God for eyes to see those in need and a heart that is moved to act and help meet those needs.

Looking at Your Life

What a model! So far you have looked at 11 of the Proverbs 31 woman's character qualities. How are you doing in growing more like her? Here are a few things to think about:

— How is your physical energy and mental determination to get things done (verse 10)?

— Can others put their trust in you (verse 11)?

— Is it your goal to help—not hurt—others (verse 12)?

— What is your attitude toward your work and chores (verse 13)?

— Do you tackle your responsibilities with energy and joy (verse 14)?

— Do you need to make any changes in your early-morning attitude (verse 15)?

— Do you have a worthy dream that you are saving your money for (verse 16)?

— Are you taking care of your health and energy so you accomplish more (verse 17)?

— Do you make it a habit to use your time well and on things that matter (verses 18 and 19)?

— How big is your heart when it comes to helping others who are in need (verse 20)?

A Prayer to Pray

Father, I'm so excited that I am understanding more about the many character qualities You want me to have and to work on. I definitely need Your help! I pray today to be committed to making these character qualities real in my daily life. Show me ways to grow more like the Proverbs 31 woman—to be more like Your ideal woman. Amen.

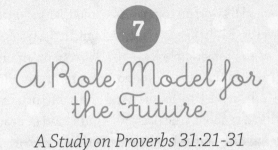

7

A Role Model for the Future

A Study on Proverbs 31:21-31

entors are something every girl, young woman, and woman needs. Whether single or married, each woman benefits from the input of someone who is more experienced, someone who can pass on wisdom to help us grow.

Well, take a look around. You are probably already surrounded by mentors. First, you have your mom. No one loves you more or cares more about you than your mother. Maybe you also have an older sister or two. At church, your girls' youth leader or youth pastor's wife may be available to you. And I'm hoping you have a loving, attentive grandmother around. She will *love* spending time with you!

But wherever you are at any time in your life, you always have the Proverbs 31 woman right in the middle of your Bible. She has stood the test of time as God's woman of excellence. You can turn to her in Proverbs 31 any time and in any place and have a visit with her. She gives you wisdom for every situation and models the many qualities God wants His women to possess—and that includes you!

Proverbs 31 is like a photo album. It is God's photo album of the remarkable Proverbs 31 woman. In Proverbs 31 you will find instruction and encouragement. You will have a role model to follow. And most important of all, you'll find out about true beauty—God's kind of beauty.

Like yummy, refreshing ice cream, let's go for another scoop. Even another bowlful! Let's return to Proverbs 31 for the conclusion of our look at this woman. Let her energy and focus stir up your heart.

Now, let's see how her story ends!

Proverbs 31:21-31

21 *She has no fear of winter for her household, for everyone has warm clothes.*

What kind of planning and preparation did this Proverbs 31 lady do for her family?

_____

_____

How did her efforts pay off for her emotionally?

_____

Personal application: The Bible tells you in many places that you are not to worry or be anxious—about anything.

But it also clearly says you should actively prepare for future events, projects, and deadlines.

What's on your schedule? Got any reports due? Any tests coming up? Are you going to audition for some special activity? Write down your most stressful upcoming challenge or responsibility.

_____

Write down steps and actions you need to take to be prepared and ready for your challenge, and do it.

_____

_____

_____

22 *She makes her own bedspreads. She dresses in fine linen and purple gowns.*

Our lady is busy—and creative! In addition to coats and cloaks of wool, what else did she make...

— for her home? _____

— for herself? _____

What is "your thing"? Your passion? Your hobby? What do you love to do most of all? Record your "thing" here.

_____

_____

A Role Model for the Future

The Proverbs 31 woman had a thing about weaving, designing, and making clothing. You'll see in a minute that her thing turned into a business! The same could happen to you as you develop your skills and talents.

23 *Her husband is well known at the city gates, where he sits with the other civic leaders.*

Meet the Proverbs 31 husband and learn a little about him. What place is mentioned?

_____

What do you learn about his character?

_____

_____

A few Bible facts: In the days of the Proverbs 31 woman, cities were walled around for protection. Gates or gated entrances containing large rooms were built into the city wall. The "elders" were the members of the government that ruled the land. They met daily in the town gate to transact any public business or judge cases or complaints that were brought before them.

24 *She makes belted linen garments and sashes to sell to the merchants.*

Meet the business side of the Proverbs 31 woman. What does she make, and what does she do with her products?

_____

_____

Do you have an avenue for earning money? Maybe you already do a little babysitting. Or maybe you take care of your neighbors' pets. Start thinking about what you are good at, what you love doing, and how you could help others out and earn a little money for your expenses, for gift-giving, church camp, hobbies, uniforms, you name it!

_____

_____

_____

25 *She is clothed with strength and dignity, and she laughs without fear of the future.*

You've heard it before: It's what's inside that counts. We've seen this woman's clothing—and it's gorgeous and magnificent. But what do you learn from this verse about her inner wear—her character?

— _____

— _____

How does her inner character affect her outlook on life?

_____

_____

Other translations of this verse read:

She shall rejoice in time to come (NKJV).

She smiles at the future (NASB).

She can laugh at the days to come (NIV).

As you look down through the corridor of time future, what are your thoughts? Dreams? Questions? Goals? Fears? What does this verse say your response should be?

_____

_____

26 *When she speaks, her words are wise, and she gives instructions with kindness.*

Who doesn't have problems with the mouth! Yet in verse 26 you learn two rules for the content your words should possess. What are they?

— _____

— _____

Bonus questions—What girl doesn't struggle with gossip? What does Proverbs 11:13 say?

A gossip _____

but those who are trustworthy _____

_____

Other verses: Three women in the Bible show us how to use our mouth in a good way. What happened when these women opened their mouths?

Mary in Luke 1:46-47—

_____

_____

Anna in Luke 2:38—

_____

_____

The older women in Titus 2:3-4—

_____

_____

27 *She carefully watches everything in her household and suffers nothing from laziness.*

Write out the two key habits seen in verse 27:

Habit 1: _____

_____

Habit 2: _____

_____

Your "household" is your personal space. Whether you have your own room or share it with a sister, you can and should "watch over" your portion of the space. And then there is your part in taking care of the rest of the place where you and your family live. Here are a few "rules to live by" that will help you to watch over your place and your extended place.

If you open it, close it.

If you turn it on, turn it off.

If you unlock it, lock it up.

If you break it, admit it.

If you can't fix it, call in someone who can.

If you borrow it, return it.

If you value it, take care of it.

If you make a mess, clean it up.

If you move it, put it back.

If it belongs to someone else, get permission to use it.[1]

Whenever you wonder, "How can I get everything done?" look again at Habit #2 of Proverbs 31:27. Write it out again and put it to work right away.

She _____

_____

28 *Her children stand and bless her. Her husband praises her:*

Here's a great use of your mouth and words! What did the children of the Proverbs 31 woman do with their mouths and words?

_____

_____

Choose to be a Proverbs 31 girl. Don't be a trouble-maker or take part in arguments. Instead, be a blessing to your parents. Honor them and do what they say. Be kind to your mom and dad every day. How hard is it to simply say, "I love you, Mom. Thanks for all you do," and "You're the best, Dad! Have a great day"? Say it, mean it, and make it a daily habit.

29 *"There are many virtuous and capable women in the world, but you surpass them all!"*

Look again at verse 28. Who is saying these words spoken in verse 29?

_____

_____

And to whom is he speaking?

_____

30 *Charm is deceptive, and beauty does not last; but a woman who fears the LORD will be greatly praised.*

It's easy to focus on outward beauty. In fact, it's almost impossible *not* to focus on outward beauty. After all, you have to look at yourself in a mirror dozens of times every day. But here in Proverbs 31:30 God gives you a "Bottom Line Beauty Tip": *"A woman who fears the LORD will be greatly praised."*

What does God say about these topics in this verse?

Charm: _____

_____

Beauty: _____

What is the source of real beauty?

_____

A few Bible facts: The writer of a Bible commentary on the book of Proverbs noted this about the woman being described: "Verse 30 is the capstone of this woman's noble character. She may be charming as well as beautiful, but her real beauty rests in her total commitment to God. Praise befits such a woman 'who fears the LORD.'"[2]

31 *Reward her for all she has done. Let her deeds publicly declare her praise.*

Look again at Proverbs 31:10, and write out the question asked there.

_____

_____

It's obvious from verse 31 that we've answered the question and found such a woman! According to the first half of verse 31, what does such a woman deserve?

_____

Wow—you did it! You scaled the heights of excellence by making your way through Proverbs 31. The woman in this chapter is God's goal for you and for me and for all of God's women.

Here are a few things from Proverbs 31:21-31 to think about as you look at your life:

— Have you added planning to your daily to-do list (verse 21)?

— Do you have a special area of interest or a hobby that challenges your creativity (verses 22 and 24)?

— Have you made a list of qualities that are important in your guy friends and also in a future husband (verses 23 and 28)?

— Are you tending to your inner beauty and character each day (verse 25)?

— What are you doing about your mouth, about gossip, about speaking with wisdom and kindness (verse 26)?

— Do you take pride in your personal space and make time to care for your possessions (verse 27)?

— Does your daily to-do list include blessing, praising, and thanking your parents (verses 28 and 29)?

— Are you spending as much time each day on

beautifying your heart in God's Word as you spend choosing your clothes and fixing your hair (verse 30)?

A Prayer to Pray

Lord, You say that the woman who loves You and follows You will be honored and praised. I want to be that kind of girl—a girl after Your own heart! I want to set my heart on You and follow in the steps of Your model of true beauty in Proverbs 31. Amen.

8

Love, Joy, and Peace

A Study on Galatians 5:22-23

Wherever you are today, I can only imagine what season of the year it is as you are reading this book. I pray every day that you are learning more about what your Bible says, about what it means, and what God wants you to do about it.

Today, as I am writing this guide to discovering the treasure that lies within the pages of your Bible, it is spring in Washington State. When I walked into the local hardware store yesterday, I was met with half a store full of tubs containing various kinds of fruit trees. They were out on display, ready to be purchased and planted with hopes that someday they would bear fruit.

Someone is going to spend a lot of time planting, fertilizing, watering, pruning, spraying, and protecting those trees until they produce fruit. As I think about those different fruit trees, I can't help but wonder about the fruit you and I are producing as Christians. I can't help but ask:

Should you and I pay any less attention to our own fruit-fulness—in our case, the spiritual kind—as these excited customers were prepared to pay attention to a mere tree?

♥ The Epistles ♥

This chapter and lesson about the "fruit of the Spirit" is found in an epistle, or letter, in the New Testament. "The epistles" begin after the book of Acts. They make up a type of literature that consists of 21 letters. These letters were written to individuals, churches, or groups of believers. They deal with every aspect of the Christian faith and your responsibilities as a Christian. It helps to approach the epistles as if you are sitting in a classroom at school and receiving instruction from one of your teachers.

The Holy Spirit Helps You Study Your Bible

There is a L-O-T of vital information shared in the epistles, so they might seem overwhelming at first. But you have help when it comes to studying and understanding the truths in your Bible. If you are a believer in Jesus Christ, God's Spirit plays several key roles in helping you understand all of the types of biblical literature. Read these verses and write out what each one teaches you about the

Holy Spirit. Also circle the different names given to the Holy Spirit.

When the Father sends the Advocate as my representative—that is, the Holy Spirit—he will teach you everything and will remind you of everything I have told you (John 14:26).

_____

_____

When the Spirit of truth comes, he will guide you into all truth (John 16:13).

_____

As you can see, the Holy Spirit gives you the ability to understand the spiritual truths of the Bible. The Spirit also provides what you need to be a girl after God's own heart. Evidence of the Holy Spirit at work in your life is revealed in what is called "the fruit of the Spirit." Read the scripture that follows and list the nine fruit, which describe what godly character looks like:

But the Holy Spirit produces this kind of fruit in our lives: love, joy, peace, patience, kindness, goodness, faithfulness, gentleness, and self-control (Galatians 5:22-23).

_____   _____   _____

_____   _____   _____

_____   _____   _____

The Fruit of the Spirit

Throughout the Bible, "fruit" refers to the outside evidence of what is on the inside. Every person who has received Jesus as Savior has the Lord living within them (1 Corinthians 6:19). God's presence is evidenced as good "fruit" or godly character. Let's learn more about each individual fruit of the Spirit. Let's see what your life will look like when you walk by the Spirit—when you exhibit the fruit of the Spirit.

You will demonstrate love—Love is self-sacrifice. Love is not merely an emotion. Love is an act of the will. In the verses that follow, how did God, the Father, and Jesus, His Son, demonstrate their love?

For this is how God loved the world: He gave his one and only Son (John 3:16).

_____

_____

Even the Son of Man [Jesus] came not to be served but to serve others and to give his life (Matthew 20:28).

_____

_____

Jesus *"resolutely set out for Jerusalem"* (Luke 9:51), where He would die for us.

_____

_____

Giving, serving, heading for Jerusalem, dying on a cross—
these are not emotional responses. They are choices and
acts of the will. They describe the kind of sacrifice Jesus
made for you and me out of love.

Personal application: How can you demonstrate love this
week toward your parents? What will you do?

_____

_____

Toward your brothers and sisters?

_____

_____

In the verse that follows, what did Jesus tell you to
do about those who clearly do not love you—about your
enemies?

*I say to you, love your enemies, bless those who curse you, do
good to those who hate you, and pray for those who...perse-
cute you* (Matthew 5:44 NKJV).

— _____

— _____

— _____

— _____

> Love involves effort, not merely emotion.
> Love demands action, not just feelings.
> Love is something you do,
> not something you only feel or say.[1]

You will display joy—When the sun is shining brightly in your life, it's easy for you to be happy. But when life turns dark and stormy and things aren't going your way, you are not quite so happy, are you? What do the verses below say to do when you experience trials and trouble?

Be thankful in all circumstances, for this is God's will for you who belong to Christ Jesus (1 Thessalonians 5:18).

_____

Dear brothers and sisters, when troubles of any kind come your way, consider it an opportunity for great joy (James 1:2).

_____

_____

Always be full of joy in the Lord. I say it again—rejoice! (Philippians 4:4).

_____

An example of joy: In the book of Nehemiah, God's people worked day and night for 52 days laboring to rebuild the ruined wall around Jerusalem. When they were finished, the Word of God was read out loud. What was the people's response? They wept as they listened. Nehemiah then encouraged the people with these words:

> The joy of the LORD is your strength!
> (Nehemiah 8:10)

Nehemiah encouraged the people of Israel not to mourn and weep, but to celebrate and be filled with joy. Why? Because they had the opportunity to listen to and understand God's Word. The same is true for you when you read your Bible. The Word of God strengthens you spiritually and brings you great joy.

The next time you feel discouraged or sad or hurt by something or someone, and you cry or you want to have a good cry, turn to God and His Word. Let the Lord strengthen you and replace your weeping with His joy.

Personal application: You will always find joy "in the Lord." Joy has nothing to do with your situation, but everything to do with your relationship with Jesus. In Jesus you can experience joy anywhere, anytime, no matter what is happening!

Write down the greatest trial or disappointment you are facing today. Whatever it is, turn to God for His joy.

Joy is not dependent on circumstances,
but on the spiritual realities of God's goodness.
Joy is not merely an emotion,
but the result of choosing to look beyond
what appears to be true in your life to
what is true about your life in Christ.[2]

You will have peace—I like to call peace "the sacrifice of trust." You make the sacrifice of trust when you face pain and stress in your life and choose to trust God instead of stressing out. Note the reason you can experience God's peace:

Don't worry about anything; instead, pray about everything. Tell God what you need, and thank him for all he has done. Then you will experience God's peace, which exceeds anything we can understand. His peace will guard your hearts and minds as you live in Christ Jesus (Philippians 4:6-7).

What is the command in verse 6?

_____

In one word, how can you keep from being anxious and worrying and experience God's peace instead?

_____

You will keep in perfect peace all who trust in you, all whose thoughts are fixed on you! (Isaiah 26:3).

According to this verse, who enjoys "perfect peace"?

— _____

— _____

[Jesus said,] "I am leaving you with a gift—peace of mind and heart. And the peace I give is a gift the world cannot give. So don't be troubled or afraid" (John 14:27).

What did Jesus promise His people before He went to the cross?

— _____

— _____

What instructions did Jesus give for receiving and experiencing His peace?

— Do not _____

— Do not _____

> Peace comes with knowing that
> Your heavenly Father is continually with you.
> Peace also comes with acknowledging that
> God will supply your every need.[3]

Isn't the Bible an amazing book! God Himself communicates to His people (and that includes you!) in the Bible, the greatest book ever written. And we are seeing that with a little reading and studying, we are beginning to understand what it means to walk by the Spirit.

Think about love, joy, and peace. These three fruit of the Spirit help you with your everyday life.

Your need for love is created when someone treats you badly, ignores you, or acts toward you with hatred. For love, look to God. His love is available—and everlasting.

Your need for joy comes when you experience sorrow, tragedy, pain, and trials. For joy, take your eyes off your pain and lift praise to God. *"Be thankful in all circumstances, for this is God's will for you who belong to Christ Jesus"* (1 Thessalonians 5:18).

Your need for peace comes as you face events in life that can cause panic, fear, terror, dread, and anxiety. You will know God's peace when you turn to Him and trust Him. The psalmist knew this truth very well: *"When I am afraid, I will put my trust in you. I praise God for what he has promised. I trust in God, so why should I be afraid?"* (Psalm 56:3-4). *"I look up to the mountains—does my help come from there? My help comes from the LORD, who made heaven and earth!"* (Psalm 121:1-2).

As you face today and every day, stay close to Jesus. Be faithful to read your Bible. Follow God's commands and walk by His Spirit. Then, when something bad happens, or your feelings are hurt, or things don't go your way, turn to God for His love, joy, and peace.

A Prayer to Pray

Father in heaven, You promised that Your Holy Spirit would be my helper—and I really need help. I know I need to show more love to my family, and I want to do that. And, as I read about joy and peace? Well, I want that too. So please help me to walk with You and be more like You. Amen.

Walking by the Spirit

A Deeper Look into the Fruit of the Spirit

*A*re you ready to continue learning more about the fruit God desires in your life? As we dive into the remaining six fruit of the Spirit, remember those we have already looked at—love, joy, and peace.

As we go on, it will help you to realize that all nine fruit stand together: Love, joy, peace, patience, kindness, goodness, faithfulness, gentleness, and self-control make up our walk with God. The fruit are like a string of Christmas lights—there is one string with many lights that, when plugged into the electrical socket, all light up at once. However, if one bulb is out of place, guess what? A lot of other lights go out too!

That's how God's fruit is brought about in our lives. When we walk by the Spirit, all of them will be evident. And when we are not walking by the Spirit, they will all go missing in our lives. Read on to see how you can display all of God's fruit in your life day by day, moment by moment.

Learning More About the Fruit of the Spirit

So far we have seen that love is willing to sacrifice itself for others. Joy praises God no matter what is happening around it. And peace trusts God with the issues of life and relaxes in His presence and promises. Now let's learn about the final six fruit of the Spirit.

You will possess patience—Patience is choosing to wait and do nothing. Patience has the ability to wait and wait—and wait...for a l-o-n-g time. Write out a dictionary definition of the word *patience*.

_____

_____

Using the same dictionary, list several words that give the opposite meaning for patience. Then circle the words that normally describe you when you have lost your patience.

_____

_____

What does the verse below tell you about the patience of God? (P.S.: It took 120 years to build the ark.)

God waited patiently while Noah was building his boat. Only eight people were saved from drowning in that terrible flood (1 Peter 3:20).

_____

_____

Personal application: What will you do the next time you need patience at home, with your family, with someone at school?

_____

_____

> Patience is a key to harmony in relationships.
> It is a practical first step to getting along with people.[1]

You will show kindness—While your patience waits and does nothing sinful (like getting mad or yelling in anger), kindness now plans for godly action.

Several months ago when I walked into my local Walmart store, my eye was immediately drawn to a large poster picturing several arrogant-looking girls standing around with some pretty awful scowls on their faces. It was an advertisement for a DVD movie being offered at a reduced price. Because I was working on this chapter on the topic of the fruit of the Spirit—more specifically on kindness—I couldn't help but react to the title of the movie: *Mean Girls 2*.

I'm guessing you know some mean girls. And I'm praying you are not a mean girl yourself! Right now contrast these mean girls and their attitudes and actions with what God asks of you.

What acts and attitudes are included in the instructions given in this verse?

Instead, be kind to each other, tenderhearted, forgiving one another, just as God through Christ has forgiven you (Ephesians 4:32).

Be _____

and _____

_____ each other,

just as _____

Love is said to be the supreme virtue that all the other fruit flow out of. In the verse below, note how kindness reveals itself.

Love is patient and kind. Love is not jealous or boastful or proud (1 Corinthians 13:4).

Love is _____

Love is not _____

We could say that kindness is an act of love, or love reveals itself in kindness.

> Kindness is the ability to love people more
> than they deserve.[2]

You will exhibit goodness—Here's a handle for under-standing goodness: Goodness does everything! In other words, goodness does everything it can to shower God's goodness and love upon others. What do the verses that follow say about goodness?

Love your enemies! Do good to those who hate you (Luke 6:27).

_____

_____

As you learned earlier from this verse, everyone has "enemies." What will you do the next time you are up against one of your enemies, up against a mean girl? What will you say? How will you act—or not act? Plan ahead and be prepared to respond in goodness.

_____

_____

_____

For we are God's masterpiece. He has created us anew in Christ Jesus, so we can do the good things he planned for us long ago (Ephesians 2:10).

_____

_____

_____

> Do all the good you can,
> by all the means you can,
> in all the ways you can,
> in all the places you can,
> at all the times you can,
> to all the people you can,
> as long as ever you can.[3]

You will act in faithfulness—which means you "just do it!" Faithfulness means choosing to do what you know you should do—what God says, no matter what. When you need to make a decision to do what's right, you don't make excuses. You won't let tiredness or laziness or any other challenge keep you from faithfully following through on your commitments and duties. Instead you look to God for His strength and then keep your word. Even with your tough decisions, God will give you everything you need to take care of your responsibilities.

In the verse that follows, underline the four qualities required in a woman who serves in her church.

Women must likewise be dignified, not malicious gossips, but temperate, faithful in all things (1 Timothy 3:11 NASB).

How many exceptions or excuses does "all things" allow for?

_____

> The hero does not set out to be one.
> Being where he was supposed to be...
> doing what he was supposed to do...
> responding as was his custom...
> to circumstances as they developed...
> devoted to duty—he did the heroic.[4]

To be a hero, look at these marks of faithfulness and determine to be more faithful:

She follows through...on whatever she has to do.

She comes through...no matter what.

She delivers the goods...whether a returned item or a school project.

She shows up...even early so others won't worry.

She keeps her word...her yes means yes and her no means no (James 5:12).

She keeps her commitments and appointments...you won't find her canceling.

She successfully transacts business...carrying out any instructions given to her.

She is regular at church...and doesn't neglect worship.

She is devoted to duty...just as Jesus was when He came to do His Father's will (John 4:34).[5]

You will exhibit gentleness—Gentleness does not mean weakness. It actually has the idea of "strength under control." A young woman who is characterized by gentleness is able to endure unkind behavior and suffering. How can she do that? She places her trust in God's wisdom, power, and love. In the eyes of others, gentleness may look like weakness, but it actually shows the greatest kind of strength! What is Jesus' promise to those who are gentle?

God blesses those who are humble [gentle, meek], for they will inherit the whole earth (Matthew 5:5).

_____

_____

Don't be concerned about the outward beauty of fancy hairstyles, expensive jewelry, or beautiful clothes. You should clothe yourselves instead with the beauty that comes from within, the unfading beauty of a gentle and quiet spirit, which is so precious to God (1 Peter 3:3-4).

What did Peter say about a woman's beauty?

Don't be concerned about _____

_____

_____

Instead _____

_____

_____

You will exhibit self-control—Self-control chooses not to think or do what you know is against God's Word. You choose not to excuse or baby yourself. You decide not to take the easy way out. You don't do something just because others are doing it so it must be okay. Instead, you say no! You say no to wrong words, thoughts, attitudes, and behaviors.

Bonus question—Look at 1 Corinthians 10:31 in your Bible. Write it out below and memorize it. Then circle the reason you should desire self-control.

_____

_____

_____

The word "self-control" means "the ability to say no."
It is an evidence of willpower that sometimes
expresses itself in "won't power."[7]

The Art of Walking

Hopefully you now have a basic understanding of the fruit of the Spirit. Well done! When you "walk by the Spirit" (Galatians 5:16 NIV), you will exhibit the fruit of the Spirit. You will exhibit godly behavior. You will be acting and responding like God would and like He tells you to respond. How is this godly behavior described in this verse?

So I say, let the Holy Spirit guide your lives. Then you won't be doing what your sinful nature craves (Galatians 5:16).

Underline God's command to you. Then write out what happens to you when you obey God's command:

_____

_____

In simple terms, walking in the Spirit means wanting to do the right thing and letting God guide you each step of the way. It means living each moment doing what God desires for you—following God with all your heart. But, as you already know, walking in the Spirit is not easy! However, Jesus has the perfect solution in John 15:5. Read on to discover the key to walking by the Spirit.

I am the vine; you are the branches. Those who remain in me, and I in them, will produce much fruit. For apart from me you can do nothing (John 15:5).

How does Jesus describe Himself?

_____

How does Jesus describe you?

_____

What happens when you don't stay close to Jesus?
Write out Jesus' exact words:

"Apart from Me _____ "

When you remain, or stay near Jesus, you will bear the
spiritual fruit of _love, joy, peace, patience, kindness, goodness, faithfulness, gentleness, and self-control._ So how do
you remain close to Jesus? Jesus has the answer:

_When you obey my commandments, you remain in my love,
just as I obey my Father's commandments and remain in his
love_ (John 15:10).

Once again, what does Jesus say is involved in staying
close to Him?

_____

Obeying God's commandments, which are found in the
Bible, is the key to walking in the Spirit.

Once again read Galations 5:16 on page 120. When you don't obey God's Word, what is the alternative action according to this verse?

_____

_____

Looking at Your Life

God wants you, as one of His children, to know Him better and better. To do this, you need to understand what God is asking of you. To know Him, you need to grow spiritually—to grow as a Christian, as a girl, as a daughter, as a sister, and as a friend. As you follow God and do what He says, you will experience spiritual growth and the fruit of His Spirit will be on display—on parade!—as you walk by the Spirit.

I thank God that you are on His path and moving forward. Just remember how simple spiritual growth is: All growth takes place one day at a time. One thought at a time. One response at a time. One decision at a time. And when you fail, stop whatever you are doing, admit your failure, confess it to God, apologize for it, and go on to greater growth.

A Prayer to Pray

Father, how I thank You for Your Word. It gives me all the answers and help I need! And I thank You for Your presence with me each day. I want to walk with You, and I want to walk in Your Spirit. I've got some changes to make, but I truly want to grow in my walk with You day by day. Amen.

10

Growing More like Jesus

Learning to Follow Him Every Day

C an you believe you did it? You made it to the end—
or at least the final chapter—of your journey into
studying your Bible! If we were face-to-face,
believe me, I'd be hugging you and giving you a big high
five, and you and I would be seriously planning a celebra-
tion, maybe a trip for pizza and ice cream.

By now you have picked up on why studying your Bible
is important. Your Bible is not just any old book from the
past. As you've looked into it for yourself and made many
life-changing applications to your life, it's become so much
more than black ink on white pages with a whole lot of
words!

No, the Bible declares countless times that it is the Word
of God. It claims to have been written by God Himself and
contains a message of utmost importance—a message
that offers life, not just for the present, but life for all eternity. This makes the Bible you hold in your hands special,

unique, one-of-a-kind, and something definitely worthy of your time, attention, and study. As you understand God's message, you gain an understanding of God Himself.

And what is God's message? The entire Bible is built around the beautiful story of Jesus Christ and His promise of eternal life for those who accept Him as God and Savior. The main reason for finding out what the Bible says is that you might understand, know, believe, and then wholeheartedly follow Jesus. This message was so important that God went ahead and spoke—to "reveal" Himself—to humanity (and you!) in His Son, the Lord Jesus Christ.

Let's look again at the Bible and see God's message about Jesus. It's a message God wants you to hear!

The Old Testament Referred to Jesus

Isaiah was one of the greatest prophets in the Old Testament. Seven hundred years before the birth of Jesus, Isaiah gave an unbelievable prophecy. Underline each description of the child that was to come.

For a child is born to us, a son is given to us. The government will rest on his shoulders. And he will be called: Wonderful Counselor, Mighty God, Everlasting Father, Prince of Peace. His government and its peace will never end. He will rule with fairness and justice from the throne of his ancestor David for all eternity (Isaiah 9:6-7).

In the New Testament, we see this prophecy come true.

Read on and underline the words that describe the fulfill-
ment of Isaiah's prediction.

*For this is how God loved the world: He gave his one and
only Son, so that everyone who believes in him will not perish but have eternal life* (John 3:16).

In 700 BC (BC refers to Before Christ), where did the
prophet Micah predict Jesus would be born?

*You, Bethlehem Ephrathah, though you are small among the
clans of Judah, out of you will come for me one who will be
ruler over Israel* (Micah 5:2 NIV).

_____

_____

_____

What does the New Testament say happened in a little town called Bethlehem—700 years after Micah's
prediction?

*Joseph...had to go to Bethlehem in Judea...He traveled
there from the village of Nazareth in Galilee. He took with
him Mary, to whom he was engaged, who was now expect-
ing a child. And while they were there, the time came for her
baby to be born* (Luke 2:4-6).

_____

_____

Personal application: Do you have trust issues when it comes to the Bible? Do you believe it is from God? Evaluate your level of trust. How do just these two fulfilled prophecies help and encourage you to believe that the Bible is the Word of God?

Why Did Jesus Come into the World?

In chapter 4 we mentioned Eve. In Genesis 3 we see what happened to Eve: She disobeyed God's one and only rule and ate the forbidden fruit. That one act of disobedience brought sin into the perfect world God created.

The world defines "sin" as no big deal—"It's nothing you need to worry about. Nothing that has any earth-shattering consequences. Hey, if it feels good, it must be okay—so go for it!"

But sin is serious! Sin is anything that is opposite to God's standards regarding what you think, say, or do. And because God is holy, He must judge sin, just as He judged Eve and Adam's sin of disobedience. So as you can see, you and I have a very big problem.

How did Jesus summarize God's standard for behavior in this verse?

Be perfect, even as your Father in heaven is perfect (Matthew 5:48).

_____

_____

_____

According to the verse below, how many people meet God's standard of perfection?

No one does good, not a single one (Romans 3:12).

_____

_____

So why did Jesus come into the world? How do these scriptures answer this question?

The Son of Man came to seek and save those who are lost (Luke 19:10).

_____

_____

Christ Jesus came into the world to save sinners (1 Timothy 1:15).

_____

_____

Why Did Jesus Have to Die?

God is Spirit and cannot die. Christ, being God, took on a body of flesh and blood to make it possible for Him to die in order to pay the price for our sins.

According to the verses that follow, what did Jesus' death accomplish?

My purpose is to give them a rich and satisfying life (John 10:10).

_____

_____

I give them eternal life, and they will never perish. No one can snatch them away from me (John 10:28).

_____

_____

Jesus' sacrifice of His life demands a personal response. According to the verses below, what must you do to become a child of God—to become a Christian?

To all who believed him and accepted him, he gave the right to become children of God (John 1:12).

My response: _____

My result: _____

Heart to heart: Have you personally received Christ as your Savior and received His payment for your sin? If you have, pause and remember the details of that life-changing decision, and thank God with all your heart. If you haven't or you aren't sure, take time now to pray. Tell God you want to know the truth, and you want to respond to it— that you want to know Jesus. Reach out and ask questions of those who can give you answers, such as your parents or a youth leader. Call out and pray to Jesus as one man did in Mark 9:24: *"Help me overcome my unbelief!"*

Jesus Is Coming Again!

Yes, it's true! The Bible says Jesus is coming again. As you read the exciting scriptures below, write out the truths and promises they contain about Jesus' return.

This same Jesus, who has been taken from you into heaven, will come back in the same way you have seen him go into heaven (Acts 1:11 NIV).

_____

_____

There is more than enough room in my Father's home. If this were not so, would I have told you that I am going to pre-pare a place for you? When everything is ready, I will come and get you, so that you will always be with me where I am (John 14:2-3).

_____

_____

_____

Growing More like Jesus

In my book *A Young Woman Who Reflects the Heart of Jesus,*[1] I focused on 12 character qualities Jesus possessed that you and I can—and should—reflect. One way to grow more like Jesus is to *want* to copy Jesus, to want to be like Him in as many ways as possible.

How can you do this? By reading about Jesus and studying His life in your Bible. This habit will change you and transform you into Jesus' image as you follow in His steps. Here are three qualities to get you started in growing more like Jesus.

Be a servant—The purpose of Jesus' life was to give—to give everything, even His very life. *"The Son of Man came not to be served but to serve others and to give his life as a ransom for many"* (Matthew 20:28). What can you do today—and every day—to be more like Jesus and be a servant at home and in public?

_____

_____

_____

Be a young woman of prayer—When you get a little extra time, look at Luke 6:12-13. There you will see Jesus praying before He made important decisions. And in Matthew 26:39-46, you will see Jesus praying as He prepares to go to the cross.

A good principle for your life—and your decision making—is, "No decision made without prayer." Even in a split second you can pray, "Lord, what is the right thing to do?" At every minute and in every situation, how does turning to God in prayer help you as seen in the verse below? (Look to the last half of this verse for the answer, starting with "so that.")

> *Let us then approach God's throne of grace with confidence, so that we may receive mercy and find grace to help us in our time of need* (Hebrews 4:16 NIV).

How are you to approach God when you pray?

_____

What happens when you turn to God in prayer?

_____

_____

Be pure—Purity doesn't just happen. You must make a decision and an effort to avoid people, places, and practices that tempt you in the wrong direction. If something tempts you to disobey God's standards, it's out! Jot down the three steps this verse gives you for staying pure:

Run from anything that stimulates youthful lusts. Instead, pursue righteous living, faithfulness, love, and peace. Enjoy the companionship of those who call on the Lord with pure hearts (2 Timothy 2:22).

Run from _____

_____

Pursue _____

_____

Have companions who _____

_____

I'm praying for you—that you will grasp how very special Jesus is as your Lord and Savior. He is the perfect model for how to live your life. Aren't you glad you have Jesus as a perfect example?

My dear reading friend, we have come to the end of this very brief, bare-bones introduction to Bible study. Way to go! You've hung in there to the end. You've wrestled with lots of technical information. And you've done the work. I wish I could give you a "Certificate of Completion." Just accept my hearty congratulations!

As we both prepare to go our separate ways, there is one really important thing I want you to remember about studying the Bible: The ultimate goal of Bible study is not to do something to the Bible. No, the ultimate goal is to have the Bible do something to you!

The purpose of Bible study is not to merely circle or underline words, or fill in blanks, or make sure you know what happened before or after a particular verse, or increase your knowledge. The purpose of Bible study is to change your life!

This is why, from page 1 of this book, I knew I wanted to end our study looking at Jesus. Loving Jesus. Rejoicing in Jesus. Worshipping Jesus. That's because the focus of the entire Bible study process is that you and I and all believers become more like Jesus. Then one glorious day we will behold Him face-to-face—and we will be like Him. The Bible tells us, *"When Christ appears...we will be like him, for we will see him as he really is"* (1 John 3:2).

A Prayer to Pray

Lord Jesus, thank You that the Bible teaches me that You are the Son of God. I love knowing I can read about You in my Bible. Help me be faithful to read and study my Bible so I can know You personally as my Savior...and as my friend. Help me walk with You every day and grow more like You. Amen.

Notes

Dedication

1. Roy B. Zuck, *The Speaker's Quote Book*, citing J. Wilbur Chapman (Grand Rapids, MI: Kregel, 1997), p. 39.

Chapter 2—First Things First

1. This quote is frequently attributed to D.L. Moody; however, the origin of it is unconfirmed.
2. *God's Words of Life for Teens* (Grand Rapids, MI: Zondervan, 2000), p. 29.

Chapter 3—A Girl After God's Heart

1. *Life Application Bible*, TLB (Wheaton, IL: Tyndale House, 1988), p. 1466.

Chapter 5—Gaining Wisdom

1. Adapted from *God's Words of Life for Teens*, NIV (Grand Rapids, MI: Zondervan, 2000), p. 45.

Chapter 6—Developing Priceless Character

1. James Strong, *Exhaustive Concordance of the Bible* (Nashville, TN: Abingdon Press, 1973), p. 39.

Chapter 7—A Role Model for the Future

1. Roy B. Zuck, *The Speaker's Quote Book* (Grand Rapids, MI: Kregel, 1997), p. 174.
2. Robert L. Alden, *Proverbs: A Commentary on an Ancient Book of Timeless Advice* (Grand Rapids, MI: Baker, 1990), p. 222.

Chapter 8—Love, Joy, and Peace

1. Elizabeth George, *A Young Woman's Walk with God* (Eugene, OR: Harvest House, 2006), p. 29.
2. George, *A Young Woman's Walk with God*, p. 41.
3. George, *A Young Woman's Walk with God*, p. 52.

Chapter 9—Walking by the Spirit

1. Elizabeth George, *A Young Woman's Walk with God* (Eugene, OR: Harvest House, 2006), p. 80.

2. Elizabeth George, *A Woman's Walk with God* (Eugene, OR: Harvest House, 2000), p. 105.

3. John Wesley, as cited in George, *A Young Woman's Walk with God*, pp. 107-8.

4. Donald K. Campbell, as cited in George, *A Woman's Walk with God*, p. 148.

5. George, *A Young Woman's Walk with God*, p. 132.

6. D.L. Moody, *Notes from My Bible and Thoughts from My Library*, quoting Bowen (Grand Rapids, MI: Baker, 1979), p. 114.

7. Dan Baumann, *Extraordinary Living for Ordinary People* (Irvine, CA: Harvest House, 1978), pp. 118-19, as cited in George, *A Young Woman's Walk with God*, p. 163.

Chapter 10—Growing More like Jesus

1. Elizabeth George, *A Young Woman Who Reflects the Heart of Jesus* (Eugene, OR: Harvest House, 2011).

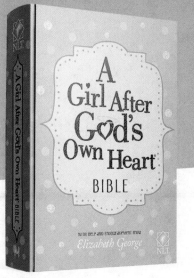

More Books by Elizabeth George

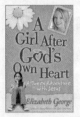

A Girl After God's Own Heart

Homework! Friends! Activities! Parents! The life of a tween girl is full of so much action—and sometimes so much *confusion*! How can I find a real best friend? How can I get along with my brothers and sisters? How can I make time in my busy life for Jesus? How can I know the right things to say and do?

As you set out on this fun adventure with Jesus, you'll learn what it means to be a girl after God's own heart. Walking with God is the most amazing journey a girl can take. Start today!

A Girl After God's Own Heart Devotional

Wouldn't you love to get advice from Someone who cares about everything you're going through? God wants to help you through good days and bad, encourage your hopes and dreams, and guide your thoughts and feelings. Through this collection of 140 fun and practical devotions, discover what God has to say—and how much He loves you!

A Girl's Guide to Making Really Good Choices

Have you ever counted how many choices you make each day? A lot!

God says that when you make good choices, your day will go so much better. You'll enjoy life a lot more and have more fun along the way.

Best of all, every good decision you make is a chance to grow closer to God, your family, and your friends. So start learning how to make the best kinds of choices...today!